THE EMERGENCY GIFT BOOK

More Than 100 Instant Gifts to the Rescue!

Potter Style

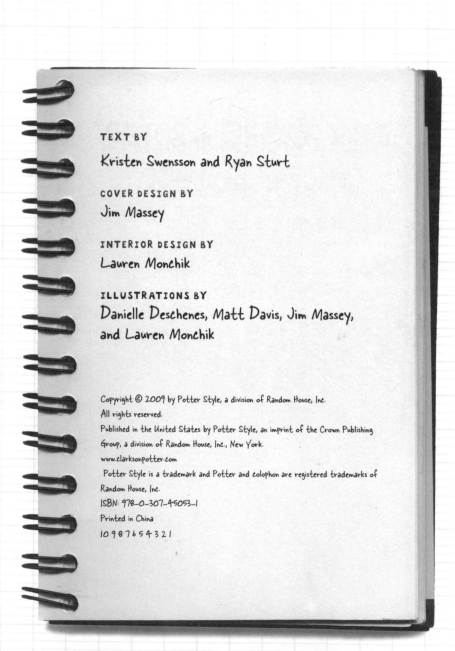

TEXT BY

Kristen Swensson and Ryan Sturt

COVER DESIGN BY

Jim Massey

INTERIOR DESIGN BY

Lauren Monchik

ILLUSTRATIONS BY

Danielle Deschenes, Matt Davis, Jim Massey,
and Lauren Monchik

Published in the United States by Potter Style, an imprint of the Crown Publishing
Group, a division of Random House, Inc., New York.
www.clarksonpotter.com
 Potter Style is a trademark and Potter and colophon are registered trademarks of
Random House, Inc.
ISBN: 978-0-307-45053-1
Printed in China
10 9 8 7 6 5 4 3 2 1

LET'S DISPENSE WITH FORMALITIES . . .

. . . and address the reasons why you might be holding this book in your hot little hands right now.

(a) You are frantically searching for a gift.

(b) You've selected about six items in this store that are just <u>perfect</u> for you, and now you are forced to contemplate a much more modest offering for someone else.

If (a) and (b) even remotely describe your situation, you have seriously found the perfect solution to your gift—giving quandary.

(c) You're hanging out and killing time while someone else does the shopping. Buying stuff just ain't your bag.

If (c) describes you more, get someone to buy this book for you. You need it desperately.

Read on . . .

So, what do we have here?

TONS AND TONS OF INSTANT, READY-MADE GIFTS FOR EVERYONE IN YOUR LIFE, FOR ALL OCCASIONS: We're pretty sure there are more than a hundred giftable items in here, and we are fairly certain that you aren't going to count them all and refute this.

FOR YOUR CONVENIENCE, THESE GIFTS ARE ALREADY ORGANIZED BY INTENDED RECIPIENT: This book is divided into "chapters" of gifts for your family, friends, roommates, lovers, and coworkers, but you don't have to abide by these designations. The boundaries that define your personal relationships are none of our concern. We are here to facilitate, not to judge.

THIS BOOK CONTAINS ALL KINDS OF IOU COUPONS: All are wallet-size and conveniently perforated. Tuck the IOU inside a card or simply hand the coupon over by itself—each one reeks of good intentions and looks handmade!

WE'VE ALSO INCLUDED SOME NOVELTY GIFTS. Like the mail-order products advertised in the back of comic books, each one promises something that is probably too good to be true (free therapy! a dog that doesn't poop! instant math skills!), but still better than nothing.

FINALLY, THERE ARE SOME REALLY INGENIOUS GIFT-CARD ENCLOSURES IN THE BACK. These are meant to gussy up generic gift cards, like the Bed, Bath & Beyond certificate that you just purchased for Mom from the rack at the pharmacy while you were picking up a 24-pack of toilet paper.

JUST THINK, ENTIRE CIVILIZATIONS HAVE BEEN BUILT ON THE NOTION OF RECIPROCITY. You'll get yours . . . but you need to kick off the process by scratching someone else's back first (or at least making a very earnest promise to do it later).

Trust us, NOTHING says "I Love You" like an IOU.

chapter 1

INSTANT GIFTS FOR YOUR PEEPS (AND CRIBMATES)

THEY KNOW YOU WELL ENOUGH NOT TO EXPECT MUCH

IN THE OLDEN DAYS OF YORE, YOUR SLACKERHOOD WAS ENDEARING.
Your pals idolized you for it, and your roommates overlooked the sloth
because you were adorable and fun—like a gigantic, occasionally hilarious
talking bunny. Alas, times have changed, bucko. Forgetting Sally's birthday
isn't quite so charmingly quirky, and your housekeeping skills are now grounds
for hitting you in the head with a hammer.

So, next time you're tempted to blow off a bud, ignore a chore list, or
shortchange your part of the brunch bill, stop. Take a deep breath. Repeat
"I am a responsible adult" three times out loud. Then flip through these pages
and punch out a present. Maybe the Fridge Restock will keep your roomie
from killing you with a rusty fork. Perhaps the Help with Your Next Move
IOU can make up for ditching your short-handed pal to play Nintendo. Heck,
there are dozens of ways to be there for a friend in need, but if you can't
hack it, you'll find a punch-out finger puppet therapist to offer instead.

REMEMBER: If you care enough to send the very best, try shopping for once
in your life. But if you're just out to prove you're not an insensitive asshat,
hand a friend one of these.

B-DAY LIST FOR YOUR A-LIST BUDS

Although this book is clearly intended to help you work around the annoyance of keeping names and dates straight, you may want to get into the practice of remembering the birthdays of a very select group of friends. Here's a page for organizing this information; for those who are intimidated by charts, we've filled one entry with a hypothetical friend* to get you started.

FRIEND'S NAME	B-DAY	QUIRKS/PREFERENCES
Lester	12/21	Loves Tequila. Thinks Shiba Inus are uppity-looking

*Note: Having trouble filling this out? chances are you're short on close friends, which means you should probably start bribing a few people. Consider handing around the stuff in this chapter immediately.

DRINKS ON ME

WOOOOO! You're old! Really old! Older than dirt, but slightly younger than God! And in honor of another wasted year, I propose we get wasted. It'll be just like the good old days, except there's a much better chance we won't get busted for fake IDs. In fact, for tonight only, the drinks are on me. AND? I'll even act as designated driver for the evening. Why? Well, I was taught to respect my elders. (As long as they don't puke in my car.)

ONE NIGHT AS YOUR WINGPERSON

Every Maverick needs a Goose, and it's time to do a fly-by over the lower to check the hot numbers cruising the runway. (Meaning: We'll go out and work as a team to help you meet somebody special.) I'll run the radio while you push the throttle and grip the joystick, baby. Let's do this.

ALL-YOU-CAN-EAT BRUNCH

Hey, since it's your birthday and all, you wanna grab some eggs? There's a great brunch place close by, and I'll spring for the whole deal. If you're into it, I'm thinking you, me, a pitcher of mimosas, three pounds of thick-cut bacon, and enough maple syrup to drown the entire population of Papua New Guinea. And if they try to serve us decaf, we cry mutiny and take the place over. Pretty sweet, right??

IOU COUPONS

for Your Peeps

To:_____

From:_____

Date:_____

Reason:_____

Date Redeemed:_____

To:_____

From:_____

Date:_____

Reason:_____

Date Redeemed:_____

To:_____

From:_____

Date:_____

Reason:_____

Date Redeemed:_____

TALK TO THE FINGER
a paper puppet therapist

Dear _____,

YOU KNOW YOU CAN TELL ME ANYTHING, RIGHT? Well, that's not entirely true. Sometimes you cross the line. My ears are open when you're stressing about slow Internet, but for bigger issues, I think a professional would come in handy. So, from now on, tell all your big, bad personal troubles to Dr. Papier here. He'll solve your problems for free, and I'll go back to watching Project Runway.

Affectionately,

HOW TO ASSEMBLE YOUR THERAPIST

1. Cut him out of this page, following the dotted line.

2. Curve the bottom band into a ring. Secure the band at your desired ring size by interlocking a top and bottom slit.

3. Slide him onto your finger and pour your heart out.

CUT SLITS   FOLD
(repeat on upper right side of band)

PLEASE PULL OUT AND TRIM ALONG DOTTED LINE

PET SITTING

I was watching Channel 11 News and was freaked out by this story of a schnauzer selling pirated software after his parents took off for a week in Rio. How quickly an animal left alone will go feral! I would hate for that to happen to your critter, so next time you go on vacation, I hereby volunteer to keep the little monster domesticated and out of your CD-R stash.

PLANT SITTING

With you out of town, I picture all of your plants looking around in dismay when the sun goes down.

Some will ask, "Wherever did the people go?" Others will answer, "Who cares? Let's raid the garbage and drink toilet water." Dirty plants. No worries, I'll watch them before they learn how to order pay-per-view.

HELP WITH YOUR NEXT MOVE

Check out these muscles. They're not just for tossing jerks out of bars, bending tire irons, or showing off on the beach.

My pythons can tape up a box of hardcover books and walk them down five flights of stairs while juggling two lamps and a birdcage, bird inside sleeping peacefully. When in need, put my guns to work on moving day.

IOU COUPONS for Your Peeps

To:_____

From:_____

Date:_____

Reason:_____

Date Redeemed:_____

To:_____

From:_____

Date:_____

Reason:_____

Date Redeemed:_____

To:_____

From:_____

Date:_____

Reason:_____

Date Redeemed:_____

IOU COUPONS for Your Peeps

IOU →

A FAVOR OF YOUR CHOOSING —

Buddy, compadre, pal o' mine, I want you to know I truly treasure our friendship, and all the great stuff you've done for me. In fact, like an awesome genie with somewhat limited powers, I'd like to repay you with any one of these three wishes.

- ☐ A ride to the airport. (So you can get the hell out of here.)
- ☐ My car for twenty-four hours. (So you can get the hell out of here.)
- ☐ A place to crash for the night. (To sleep if you can't get the hell out of here.)
- ☐ Bonus Option _____

Just submit this signed voucher (or text me if that's easier) and your wish is my command.

TECHNICAL ASSISTANCE FOR MY FAVORITE TECHNOPHOBE

I look at your place with all that gear sitting around unappreciated, collecting dust instead of electrons, their potential never to be actualized, and to me

it's like the island of misfit toys. If only someone would show them how wonderful they truly are! Do not fret! I'm here like a little cobbler elf in the night. In a flurry of wires and wild button mashing, you will have a setup that is seriously set up. Try not to break it.

MULTIPLE-CHOICE TREAT

Thank you for being a friend! We've traveled down the road and back again. My heart is true, and in your honor, I'll pay for any of the following.

- ☐ A film of your choosing. (French films included. They're so enchantingly blasé!)
- ☐ A meal at the restaurant of your choice. (Indian included, even though it makes me fart.)
- ☐ A massage at the spa of your choice. (Pricey ones included. Maybe they'll even throw in some hot tea.)
- ☐ A tooth extraction at the dentist of your choice. (Novocain not included. Sorry. That stuff's expensive.)

I. O. U.

IOU COUPONS

for Your Peeps

To:_____

From: _____

Date: _____

Reason: _____

Date Redeemed:_____

To:_____

From: _____

Date: _____

Reason: _____

Date Redeemed:_____

To:_____

From: _____

Date: _____

Reason: _____

Date Redeemed:_____

WRISTBAND OF ROYALLY AWESOME POWER

Let them hear you sing! Putting this wristband on gives power to say and do whatever, and everybody has to listen to your soliloquies. (It has a built-in jerk fuse, so don't blow it by being a douche.)

WRISTBAND OF THE PUPPET MASTER

With this mighty instrument you may command someone to do just about anything: run and get coffee, perform a sketch show, build a jet, see God, whatever. (Pretty mighty! But if you're not nice, the power disappears—so use wisely!)

WRISTBAND OF SERENDIPITY

Wear this band and suddenly your day is filled with unexpected pleasures. (Make sure everybody knows you're putting it on WAY ahead of time. No reason. Just, that's how its magic works. I guess.)

WRISTBAND OF THE PARTY ANIMAL

O damned day! The wearer of this bestial magic item is doomed to have fun whilst all responsibilities and expenses for the debauchery are placed on the shoulders of one's oh-so-fortunate companions!

My dear
friend

_____,

**THESE
ENCHANTED
WRIST-
BANDS**
come with
some special
conditions.
To activate,
punch each
one cleanly
out of this
page. Each
band is good
for a single
twenty-
four-hour
period,
after which
it is com-
pletely null
and void.
You must be
wearing the
wristband
in some
fashion in
order to
realize your
full power.
Get creative
and enjoy
the privi-
ledges of
absolute
sovereignty.

NAME OF WEARER:

DATE/TIME ACTIVATED:

DATE/TIME EXPIRED:

NAME OF WEARER:

DATE/TIME ACTIVATED:

DATE/TIME EXPIRED:

NAME OF WEARER:

DATE/TIME ACTIVATED:

DATE/TIME EXPIRED:

NAME OF WEARER:

DATE/TIME ACTIVATED:

DATE/TIME EXPIRED:

CAN'T DO SEVENTH-GRADE MATH

a wallet-size calculator —just for you

Dear _____,

OH, HONEY. Math is hard. I know. And I know it's especially difficult when there's a bunch of impatient friends staring testily at you, expecting you to magically calculate an 18 percent tip off a $74.88 restaurant bill. Before you fling yourself screaming and crying out a window, try this calculator. It'll make your life (and ours) a LOT easier.

Warmest Wishes,

_____

CHECK	15%	20%	CHECK	15%	20%
$1.00	$0.15	$0.20	$26.00	$3.90	$5.20
2.00	0.30	0.40	27.00	4.05	5.40
3.00	0.30	0.40	28.00	4.20	5.60
4.00	0.60	0.80	29.00	4.35	5.80
5.00	0.75	1.00	30.00	4.50	6.00
6.00	0.90	1.20	31.00	4.65	6.20
7.00	1.05	1.40	32.00	4.80	6.40
8.00	1.20	1.60	33.00	4.95	6.60
9.00	1.35	1.80	34.00	5.10	6.80
10.00	1.50	2.00	35.00	5.25	7.00
11.00	1.65	2.20	36.00	5.40	7.20
12.00	1.80	2.40	37.00	5.55	7.40
13.00	1.95	2.60	38.00	5.70	7.60
14.00	2.10	2.80	39.00	5.85	7.80
15.00	2.25	3.00	40.00	6.00	8.00
16.00	2.40	3.20	41.00	6.15	8.20
17.00	2.55	3.40	42.00	6.30	8.40
18.00	2.70	3.60	43.00	6.45	8.60
19.00	2.85	3.80	44.00	6.60	8.80
20.00	3.00	4.00	45.00	6.75	9.00
21.00	3.15	4.20	46.00	6.90	9.20
22.00	3.30	4.40	47.00	7.05	9.40
23.00	3.45	4.60	48.00	7.20	9.60
24.00	3.60	4.80	49.00	7.35	9.80
25.00	3.75	5.00	50.00	7.50	10.00

TIP TRANSLATOR

Learning good tipping etiquette is like learning another language. *Biggledee bloo blar fnar tip!* Here's a quick translator to let you know what your server hears when you slap down the cash.

10% TIP: I remember when coffee was a nickel! You'll take my tip and like it!

15% TIP: Mediocrity becomes you. I coldly thank you for being adequate.

20% TIP: In some countries a loud belch is a compliment. *BUUURRRRP!* (in a good way!)

20%+ TIP: All my troubles evaporated after that meal and your incredible service. Here is my firstborn.

no TIP: I just heard that everything I own has been utterly destroyed by a freak meteor crash. Such is my excuse.

PLEASE PULL OUT AND TRIM ALONG DOTTED LINE

CHECK	15%	20%	CHECK	15%	20%
$51.00	$7.65	$11.20	**$76.00**	$11.40	$15.20
52.00	7.80	11.40	**77.00**	11.55	15.40
53.00	7.95	11.40	**78.00**	11.70	15.40
54.00	8.10	11.80	**79.00**	11.85	15.80
55.00	8.25	12.00	**80.00**	12.00	16.00
56.00	8.10	12.20	**81.00**	12.15	16.20
57.00	8.55	12.40	**82.00**	12.30	16.40
58.00	8.70	12.60	**83.00**	12.45	16.60
59.00	8.85	12.80	**84.00**	12.60	16.80
60.00	9.00	13.00	**85.00**	12.75	17.00
61.00	9.15	13.20	**86.00**	12.90	17.20
62.00	9.30	13.40	**87.00**	13.05	17.40
63.00	9.45	13.60	**88.00**	13.20	17.60
64.00	9.60	13.80	**89.00**	13.35	17.80
65.00	9.75	13.00	**90.00**	13.50	18.00
66.00	9.90	13.20	**91.00**	13.65	18.20
67.00	10.05	13.40	**92.00**	13.80	18.40
68.00	10.20	13.60	**93.00**	13.95	18.60
69.00	10.35	13.80	**94.00**	14.10	18.80
70.00	10.50	14.00	**95.00**	14.25	19.00
71.00	10.65	14.20	**96.00**	14.40	19.20
72.00	10.80	14.40	**97.00**	14.55	19.40
73.00	10.95	14.60	**98.00**	14.55	19.60
74.00	11.10	14.80	**99.00**	14.85	19.80
75.00	11.25	15.00	**100.00**	15.00	20.00

IOU COUPONS for Your Peeps

ONE NIGHT OF BREAKUP RECOVERY

Lame. LAME. LAAAAAAAAAME. Breaking up with you is the lamest thing Dolty McSimpleton has ever done. But hey: forget Nitwit O'Dumbell. You're too good for that crap, and things will be infinitely better with Loony Lamebrain-D'Imbecile in the rearview mirror. In fact, tonight we'll hit the town so hard, you'll forget all about Dullard Moronella. Some kind of Hottie McAttractivitz will pop up on your radar, and love will rule once more.
→ IOU ←

AN APOLOGY

I'm sorry. SO sorry. There has never been anyone sorrier in the history of man, space, or time. I can't believe I was so colossally stupid and:

- ☐ Ditched you that morning/night/Arbor Day.
- ☐ Dated that loudmouth/buffoon/ex of yours.
- ☐ Opened my big, fat mouth/jaw/butt.
- ☐ Stained your shirt/car/puppy.
- ☐ Generally was a terrible friend/pal/ex-bestie.
- ☐ All of the above.

 ## TLC WHEN YOU FEEL LIKE SH—T

We've all been there: curled on the couch in a feverish ball, desperately clawing at Puffs Plus, lest our nasal drippings soak our pajamas like some terrible, germ-infested polyester sponge. Being sick sucks, yo. And on those awful days we wished our sinuses never existed, there's nothing more welcome than a good friend bearing chicken soup and Mucinex. Hear this: The next time you contract the plague, I will be that good friend. Just don't sneeze on me.

IOU COUPONS for Your Peeps

To:_____

From:_____

Date:_____

Reason:_____

Date Redeemed:_____

To:_____

From:_____

Date:_____

Reason:_____

Date Redeemed:_____

To:_____

From:_____

Date:_____

Reason:_____

Date Redeemed:_____

DARLING FUSS-FREE PET

Dear _____,

I KNOW THAT YOU'VE ALWAYS WANTED A DOG, but are you seriously ready for that level of responsibility? Meet Mr. Folders, a rare miniature breed from the Pulp Islands who'll be your faithful friend for life. Doesn't eat, completely hypoallergenic, no training necessary, and zero poop to clean up or step in! Say hi to a dependent. you can depend on who won't depend on you. (But if you lose this creature it will haunt you forever. Such is its curse!) Your best friend, _____.

HOW TO BRING YOUR PET TO LIFE

1. Neatly trim along outline of dog.

2. Fold limbs, neck, head, ears, and tail along dotted lines.

3. Customize your critter with sticker accessories (see next page).

trim

fold

fold

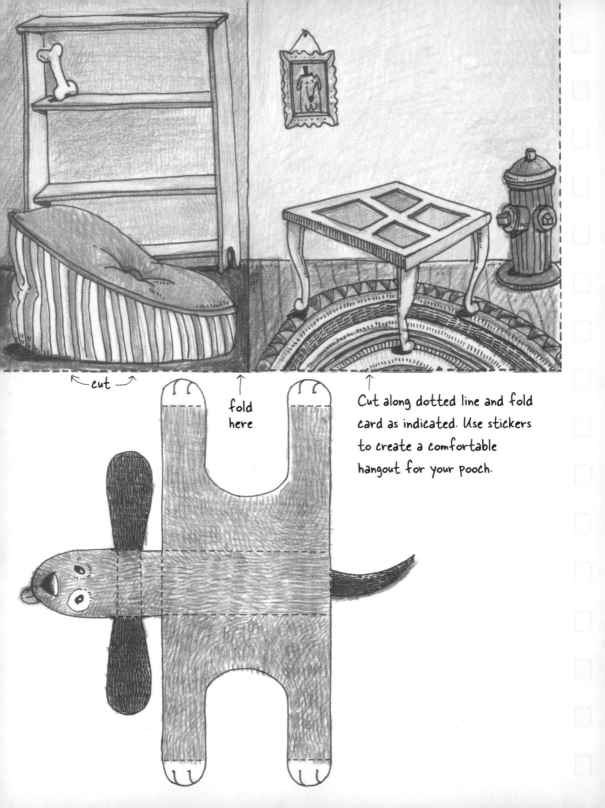

← cut →

fold
here

Cut along dotted line and fold
card as indicated. Use stickers
to create a comfortable
hangout for your pooch.

PAPER POOCH ACCESSORIES

Choose your pooch's personality . . .

Select your pooch's sweater . . .

 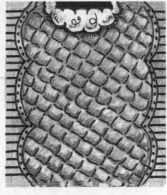 

Give your pooch some boots . . .

    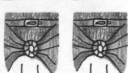

Outfit the pooch pad . . .

IOU COUPONS for Your Cribmates

DIRTY DISH DUTY

There comes a time in every young person's life when they have to cast old habits asunder, suck it up, and become an adult. For me, my friend, that day is today. So move aside! Clear the way! Don't try to stop me!

Because . . . yes, the rumors are true. I'm doing the dishes—mine AND yours. All you have to do is fill the sink and trust me to fulfill my destiny.

BATHROOM CLEANING

Long, long ago in a suburban town far, far away, my mother taught me the ways of Clorox, Ajax, and Windex. And while this is the first time I've ever realized that all bathroom cleaners end in "x," it isn't the first time I'll have cleaned a bathroom. So name the time and place and I'll be there, toilet brush in hand.

I.O.U. → GARBAGE DUTY

One man's trash is another man's treasure. Let's look at what we got here. Enough old bills to papier-mâché a dinosaur. Plenty of food scraps for a compost heap. A cereal box hat. A sock that can surely be upcycled into a puppet. And are you seriously throwing away a Buster Poindexter CD? He's genius! Know what? I'll take out the garbage. No, it's cool. I got it.

IOU COUPONS
for Your Cribmates

To:_____

From:_____

Date:_____

Reason:_____

Date Redeemed:_____

To:_____

From:_____

Date:_____

Reason:_____

Date Redeemed:_____

To:_____

From:_____

Date:_____

Reason:_____

Date Redeemed:_____

COHABITATION MERIT BADGES

Encourage your roommate to collect them all.

You've got the skillz to split the billz.

Slayer of many legs.

For wiring and clicking wizardry.

We'd wallow in trash without you.

For keeping it clean.

Thanks to you, we have furniture.

IOU COUPONS for Your Cribmates

FRIDGE RESTOCK

Agent X: Many apologies for infiltrating your food supply. It couldn't be avoided.

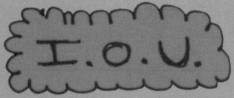

Sustenance designated for the colonel's pet project was running low, compromising the entire mission. Operation Monkey Ballerina appreciates your sacrifice and will reconstitute your stash once the budget has been approved by the Pentagon. That established, please know this IOU will self-destruct in ten seconds, barring unforeseen technical errors by Bob in IT. Sincerely, Agent Q

AN ALCOHOL RESTOCK

Attention shoppers, we have a giant spill in aisle three. Beer, wine, and liquor are all over the freaking place, and the shelves are now empty. Do not panic. Please refrain from yelling. We do not need volunteers to mop. The aisle is closed until we can restock the shelves—which we will do immediately to avoid a full-scale riot. (Sorry for draining the supply, I'll refill it.)

MONEY FOR UTILITIES

I can barely see you in this candlelight, but I'm sure you can smell me from there. (Oh, what a difference a warm shower makes.) No electric, no heat, no water. Nothing like roughing it, right? Ha-ha. Ahem.

Nice sleeping bag. Anyway, so I guess maybe needing a campfire in the living room is kind of a horrible idea, so I'll just give you the overdue money for my share of the bills, mmkay?

IOU COUPONS for Your Cribmates

To:_____

From:_____

Date:_____

Reason:_____

Date Redeemed:_____

To:_____

From:_____

Date:_____

Reason:_____

Date Redeemed:_____

To:_____

From:_____

Date:_____

Reason:_____

Date Redeemed:_____

FRIDGE PATROL STICKIES

Dear _____,
    (name of cohabitant)

I HEREBY APPOINT YOU the CFO (Chief Food Organizer) of our refrigerator. After all, you're the one who goes batshit when we end up with seven open jars of pasta sauce. These stickers will aid you in your official duties.

THIS GAVE ME GAS BUT I HATE TO THROW OUT OTHERWISE PERFECTLY GOOD FOOD, SO HELP YOURSELF.

_____'s **Leftovers**
☐ **Help yourself!**
☐ **Do Not Touch**

_____'s **Leftovers**
☐ **Help yourself!**
☐ **Do Not Touch**

OMG, WTF IS IN THIS TUPPERWARE? PLEASE DESTROY BEFORE IT ESCAPES AND TAKES OVER A MAJOR FINANCIAL INSTITUTION.

STOP RIGHT THERE! I KNOW EXACTLY HOW MANY _____ ARE LEFT IN HERE, SO DON'T EVEN TRY TO SIPHON OFF ANOTHER ONE.

UP FOR GRABS!

SOMETHING STINKS.

Like a rotten egg laid by a diseased chicken. I'm pretty sure the culprit is in this container.

Homemade by _____'s Mom
World-famous recipe for_____
And no, I'm not sharing.

OK, THIS IS THE ____ TIME I'VE BOUGHT THIS FOR THE HOUSE. JUST LETTING Y'ALL KNOW.

HAVE YOURSELF A NAKED DAY

Dear _____,
(name of roommate)

THE GIFT OF COMPLETE PRIVACY IS ALL YOURS, WITH THIS HANDY GET-THE-HELL-OUT-OF-HERE DOORKNOB SIGN.

For eight straight hours of your choosing, I will make myself scarce so that you can do whatever the heck you want—in any room you want—without fear of roommate interruptus. No questions asked, believe me.

Yours in cohabitation,

_____

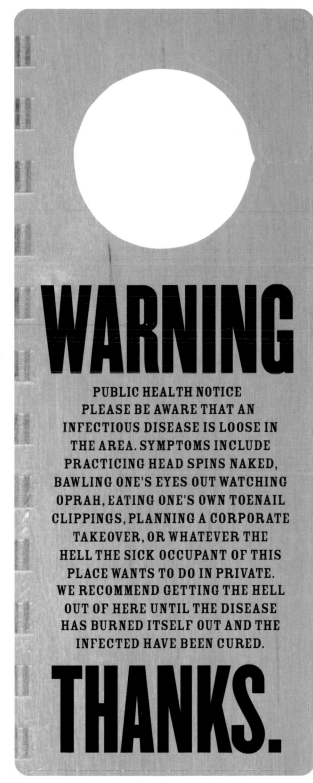

WARNING

PUBLIC HEALTH NOTICE PLEASE BE AWARE THAT AN INFECTIOUS DISEASE IS LOOSE IN THE AREA. SYMPTOMS INCLUDE PRACTICING HEAD SPINS NAKED, BAWLING ONE'S EYES OUT WATCHING OPRAH, EATING ONE'S OWN TOENAIL CLIPPINGS, PLANNING A CORPORATE TAKEOVER, OR WHATEVER THE HELL THE SICK OCCUPANT OF THIS PLACE WANTS TO DO IN PRIVATE. WE RECOMMEND GETTING THE HELL OUT OF HERE UNTIL THE DISEASE HAS BURNED ITSELF OUT AND THE INFECTED HAVE BEEN CURED.

THANKS.

PUBLIC HEALTH NOTICE

ALL TRACES OF THE INFECTION
HAVE DISAPPEARED, AND ALL IS
WELL WITH THE WORLD. YOU MAY
ENTER THE PREMISES ONCE AGAIN.
FEEL FREE TO FROLIC AND REJOICE
ALL OVER THE PLACE.

THANKS.

chapter 2

INSTANT GIFTS FOR YOUR SIGNIFICANT OTHER

AWW . . . YOU'RE SO CUTE WHEN YOU MAKE AN EFFORT

WHEN IT COMES TO RELATIONSHIPS, YOU'RE A CHAMP. You say all the right things, you make all the right moves, and you don't dress too shabby either. Actually, you'd date yourself if you were available.

Still, there's one niggling thing that keeps you and . . . well, you . . . from having the perfect union. You're not the world's greatest gift giver.

It started small: an inappropriate card here, a last-minute stuffed flamingo there. Nothing too crazy. But if you buy one more lame-ass foot massager (or worse, forget a present altogether), you'll be tarred, feathered, and berated until your self-esteem is a distant memory.

Never fear, though. The following pages are chock-full of stuff to save the day. The Two-Week Compromise on Household Cleanliness might be enough to send your SO into a dither. If not, a Date Night In could change the way you see each other (naked). And if that doesn't work, the origami Diamond Ring will tide your lover over until you can get your dirty hands on a real one.

Whatever you decide, make sure to punch out an Instant Apology. Odds are you'll need it anyway.

THE STATS ON YOUR SQUEEZE

How much do you really know about that special someone in your life? Intimate details like shoe size, allergies, and a preference for natural fibers may all come into play when selecting a gift, so start paying attention. Some people are sensitive—or not entirely honest—when asked about things like their clothing sizes. If your lover isn't entirely forthcoming, try going through his/her closet, drawers, and garbage can, and take very specific notes.

SHIRT SIZE:

PANTS SIZE:

DRESS SIZE:

INTIMATE APPAREL SIZES:

SHOE SIZE:

SIGNATURE SCENT:

FAVORITE COLORS:

FAVORITE SWEET:

DRINK OF CHOICE:

FAVORITE FLOWER:

OTHER INDULGENCES/VICES:

UNFORTUNATE ALLERGIES:

IOU COUPONS

A TWO-WEEK COMPROMISE ON HOUSEHOLD CLEANLINESS

Is the house half–clean or is it half–dirty? It all depends on your perspective. I'm willing to put all of my annoying lifelong habits aside and see things your way, so however you define "clean" is cool with me for the next two weeks. I say "toe–may–toe" stain, you say "toe–mah–toe" stain. Let's call the whole thing off.

I.O.U.

DATE NIGHT IN

Hey, baby. You know you want me. What's more, you know you want me in the comforts of our own home, over a fine meal of takeout sushi and Boone's Strawberry Hill. So sit back while I dim the lights, jack up the Barry White, and put on some clean undies. I promise: This will be the night in you've always dreamed about (minus Brad Pitt and/or Angelina Jolie . . . hey, I don't know what you're into).

I.O.U.

DATE NIGHT OUT

Baby, you know how much I love sittin' on the couch, watching Biggest Loser and eating cereal straight from the box. I love it almost as much as reading in bed and watching you play video games. Still, I feel like we need to get out there—to experience our love as it was meant to be experienced, in something dressier than our underwear. So what say you and me hit the town? My treat.

I.O.U.

IOU COUPONS
for Your Significant other

To:_____

From: _____

Date: _____

Reason: _____

Date Redeemed:_____

To:_____

From: _____

Date: _____

Reason: _____

Date Redeemed:_____

To:_____

From: _____

Date: _____

Reason: _____

Date Redeemed:_____

NEXT HOLIDAY WITH YOUR FAMILY  I.O.U.

My family's going to Vegas for the holiday. First-class tickets, twenty years of credit card rewards, tickets to Elton, and a penthouse suite at the tippy top of the Luxor. They'll be pharaohs for the weekend, basking in glory. Too bad for them their prodigal child has other plans. That's right, slap on the sweater vest and pack the PJs (the ones with the footies), because next holiday? We're putting in some bona fide bonding time with your family. Vegas can wait.

AN INTIMATE EVENING

Sweetheart, we have two options tonight. We can drink tea and play a lovely game of Parcheesi at the local library, or we can get DIZZOWN and DIRTY with our sweet, naked-ass selves. Picture it: you, me, a few candles, and a squeeze bottle of Hershey's chocolate syrup. Because by the end of the night, you'll be my own personal sundae (*wink*).

AN APOLOGY: FOR FORGETTING A VERY IMPORTANT DATE

Sweetheart, I messed up. I forgot our anniversary, and for that I'm an idiot. A jerk. A moron of the highest order. And now I'm asking—nay, BEGGING—for your mercy. Because I may be scum, but YOU are kind and benevolent and smart and hot and generally the greatest lover on the face of the earth. And if you forgive me, I'll try to be half the person you are. Promise.

IOU COUPONS

for Your Significant Other

To:_____

From:_____

Date:_____

Reason:_____

Date Redeemed:_____

To:_____

From:_____

Date:_____

Reason:_____

Date Redeemed:_____

To:_____

From:_____

Date:_____

Reason:_____

Date Redeemed:_____

INSTA-BLING!

INSTANT DIAMOND RING

My Sweet _____,

WHEN IT COMES TO LOVE, ISN'T SENTIMENT WORTH MORE THAN SHELLING OUT A TON OF DOUGH? Doesn't affection trump expense? Wouldn't you rather have a modest origami ring over a tricked-out diamond monstrosity? You would, right? RIGHT? Please say yes. Because if you do, I have just the jewelry in mind.

Yours always,

_____

HOW TO ASSEMBLE YOUR RING

1. Cut out around dotted line.

2. Fold top and bottom edges of the band back, following the fold lines.

3. Trim one end along dotted line.

4. Bend band into a ring and tuck curved end into the open slit on the other end. Done!

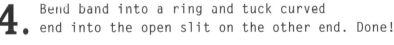

1.

2.

4.

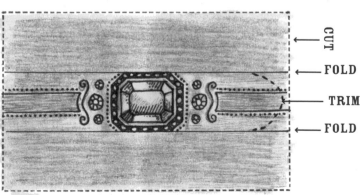

← CUT

← FOLD

← TRIM

← FOLD

AN APOLOGY: FOR BEING A WORKAHOLIC

Some people work for the financial rewards. Others do it so they're contributing members of society. Still others work out of ambition, as nothing would be worse than failing to fulfill their intellectual promise. Me? I work because my office chair is comfy, and sometimes I forget what time it is. But I promise: my hours will get better, and I'll make up the time that we missed together. In other words, I'll work on us.

AN APOLOGY: FOR COMING HOME SO DRUNK

Last night? Well, my alcohol tolerance was low from the single pea I had for dinner. Those breath mints must have done something to my body chemistry. My water got mixed up with water-flavored vodka. I felt a drip during karaoke, and when I looked up a pint of lager went in my mouth, Carrie-style. The taxi driver made me do tequila shots as my fare. Outside the house a caterpillar gave me a bottle that said DRINK ME, and who can argue with a caterpillar? It was all a huge misunderstanding, but let me take you to brunch.

AN APOLOGY: FOR BEING A NAG ⟵   I . O . U .

Nagging is an art form. It takes deep thought and relentless practice to pull off well. There are few truly great nags throughout history, and even then, only some can be considered canonical. Perhaps you can tell, but it's been my solemn and constant wish to enter this pantheon. While this pursuit of greatness is profoundly noble, I acknowledge it's also annoying as hell. You're meant to be my partner, not my victim. I apologize for the inadvertent irritation.

IOU COUPONS

for Your Significant other

To:_____

From:_____

Date:_____

Reason:_____

Date Redeemed:_____

To:_____

From:_____

Date:_____

Reason:_____

Date Redeemed:_____

To:_____

From:_____

Date:_____

Reason:_____

Date Redeemed:_____

MAGICAL WRISTBANDS FOR LOVERS

WORK BUT ONCE, AND FOR ONE DAY ONLY!

WRISTBAND OF THE WARDROBE WARLORD

The giver of this device must obey the fashion wishes of its wearer. You are the puppet master! (Use this VERY wisely!)

WRISTBAND OF THE MUSIC LORD

Rock on! No fool dare veto the music choices made by whoever wears this modest adornment. (Only works in cars. *Such is its curse!*)

WRISTBAND OF THE ROAD WARRIOR

Decide where this vehicle goes and the driver will accelerate, brake, and merge as you instruct. BUT, if *you* take the wheel, passenger-side driving will be violently SILENCED.

WRISTBAND OF THE TV WIZARD

You are hereby ordained to decide what's on TV so long as you wear this. The remote control is powerless in any other hand but yours. Now, make your choice!

Dearest

_____,

**THESE
WRIST-
BANDS**
aren't just
for show.
Sure, you'll
look pretty
fierce
wearing one,
but here's
the real
gift: Each
one grants
you ABSOLUTE
POWER over
one aspect
of our two-
person
universe
for exactly
twenty-four
hours. Go
ahead—rule
my world.

All yours,

_____

NAME OF WEARER: _____
DATE/TIME ACTIVATED: _____
DATE/TIME EXPIRED: _____

NAME OF WEARER: _____
DATE/TIME ACTIVATED: _____
DATE/TIME EXPIRED: _____

NAME OF WEARER: _____
DATE/TIME ACTIVATED: _____
DATE/TIME EXPIRED: _____

NAME OF WEARER: _____
DATE/TIME ACTIVATED: _____
DATE/TIME EXPIRED: _____

TIME TO TALK

So, you know that . . . thing . . . you keep wanting to talk about? The one where you bring it up, and I change the subject, because it's monumentally uncomfortable? Well, I'm ready now. Let's discuss. Let's have a conversation. Let's gab until our tongues fall out, and we have to gum all our meals for the rest of our lives. And if I get twitchy, feel free to slap me upside the head. Think of it as a bonus.

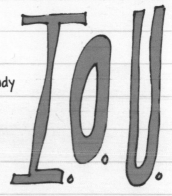

A CONFESSION OF AFFECTION

Hi. You're cute. Exactly how cute? Well, let's see . . .

- [ ] No continent on the planet is shaped like your face, and that sucks.
- [ ] I'd paint a portrait of you, but I'm afraid of art thieves stealing it.
- [ ] You are cuter than a dozen kittens meowing songs written by puppies.
- [ ] No photo does you justice, except that one with a

million turning heads stopping traffic worldwide.

— ANOTHER CONFESSION OF AFFECTION — —

Hi. I like you. I like you so much that:

- [ ] I would name the castle I built with my bare hands after you.
- [ ] If my feelings were a rhinoceros, they would charge only you, but with love.
- [ ] I want to put you in my hat so you could secretly see my life all the time.
- [ ] You make me blush, even when I'm alone, in space, and the communicator is off.
- [ ] My feelings for you run on a treadmill that actually goes to great places.

IOU COUPONS
for Your Significant other

To:_____

From:_____

Date:_____

Reason:_____

Date Redeemed:_____

To:_____

From:_____

Date:_____

Reason:_____

Date Redeemed:_____

To:_____

From:_____

Date:_____

Reason:_____

Date Redeemed:_____

IOU COUPONS
for Your Significant other

ONE WEEK OF NO COMPLAINING

I complain. I freely admit this. I know it's occasionally unmerited, and some days I would make the Dalai Lama want to stab me with a letter opener. I'm working on it though. I'm trying to look at the silver lining instead of the rainy grayness contained within.

So, how about this: I promise to go seven days without whining uncontrollably. You pick the week, and I'll start working on that glass—half—full thing.

ONE WEEK OF CHORES AND ERRANDS

Welcome to the robot of the fuuuuuuture. I'm Robotic Assistant GSD-9000, your servant for one whole week. Laundry? Watch me fold! In the kitchen I make automatic dinners, dishes washed and dried. Think of the time savings! The robot of the future does it all, unobtrusively picking up the house, running errands, cooking, and cleaning so you have time to focus on the important stuff this week. Stupendous! (*Batteries not included, but please don't try to put any in.)

A LONG MASSAGE

You're a hottie. There. I said it. You're unbelievably attractive, and you make me wanna swoon, sweat, and shoop all at the same time. I drool openly when you flex, and when we're food shopping, it's all I can do to avoid feeling you up in the cereal aisle. In fact, my wildest dream involves you, a gazebo in Maine, and four gallons of Jif. For now, though, how about a massage? We'll work our way up to the peanut butter thing later.

IOU COUPONS

for Your
Significant
other

To:_____

From:_____

Date:_____

Reason:_____

Date Redeemed:_____

To:_____

From:_____

Date:_____

Reason:_____

Date Redeemed:_____

To:_____

From:_____

Date:_____

Reason:_____

Date Redeemed:_____

chapter 3

INSTANT GIFTS FOR YOUR FAMILY

NOTHING SAYS "I LOVE YOU" LIKE SAYING "I LOVE YOU" (AN IOU IS GOOD TOO)

MOM HAS ALL THE CHRISTMAS TREE ORNAMENTS SHE NEEDS. Dad's set for life with golf balls. Grandma keeps repeating "Really dear, we don't need anything," like it's the family motto. Still, you know you have to get your parents, grandparents, and siblings SOMETHING. Otherwise, you'll be ostracized like Cousin Kim, who didn't send Grandpa a gift one year and was never heard from again.

How about lending Mom your services as Maid for a Day? She'll appreciate the vacuuming much more than another puffy wolf sweatshirt. And really, couldn't Dad use a Wardrobe Update? It beats the ever-loving crap out of a third omelet pan. (Speaking of which—who buys their father three omelet pans? Cool Hand Luke can't eat that many eggs.) As for Grandma and Grandpa, isn't it time you sat down and listened to their Life Stories? They've been waiting to relive the war years since . . . well, the war.

See, your family loves you, and they want to be acknowledged. And there's no better way to acknowledge them than by slipping them a piece of paper that promises them they'll soon be acknowledged. Got that? Good.

THE DAMN FAMILY

OK, so you're pretty much expected to know your mom and dad's birthday, and probably your siblings too. But the American family is a complex organism these days. People come and go; they get married, get divorced, reproduce, and acquire stepchildren. Nothing says "Lucky you, you're still one of us!" like remembering a relative's special day, so we're offering you an opportunity to keep track here.

RELATION	B-DAY	HAS HE/SHE ACKNOWLEDGED MY B-DAY?	
Mom's partner/spouse:		__Yes	__No
Dad's partner/spouse:		__Yes	__No
Step-Siblings:		__Yes	__No
		__Yes	__No
		__Yes	__No
		__Yes	__No
		__Yes	__No
Step-Grandparents:		__Yes	__No
		__Yes	__No
		__Yes	__No
		__Yes	__No
Various In-laws / Others:		__Yes	__No
		__Yes	__No
		__Yes	__No
		__Yes	__No

IOU COUPONS for Mom

A NIGHT ON THE TOWN

There are so many things I could have purchased for your birthday, Mom. Alas, flowers die, chocolates melt, and George Clooney threatened to take out a restraining order if I kept hanging around his mansion. So instead, I got you the gift that keeps on giving: me. In the next few weeks, you and I will spend three, four, or maybe even FIVE hours together doing whatever you want. And I will pay for it. (What? I will. Stop laughing.)

MAID FOR A DAY

I've known you for awhile now, Mom, and in all that time, I've never known you to want anything more than a clean house. Love, money, faith in humanity: to you, these things are wonderful concepts, but you'd gladly sacrifice any one for a dust-free living room or a sink blessedly lacking in dirty dishes. So, this year, for your birthday, BECAUSE I LOVE YOU, I'm making the ultimate sacrifice. I will be your maid for one whole day. 12 hours. Do what you will. I'm pretty sure I can take it.

i.o.u.

HOMEMADE DINNER ON ME

Mom, thinking of you makes me want to stuff my face. And call me crazy, but I'm pretty sure you feel the same. So, how about we do it together? On the evening of your choosing, I'll cook us a dinner so tasty and opulent, every meal for the rest of your life will pale in comparison. (Even chicken enchiladas.) Sound good? Excellent. I'll bring the groceries and multiple bottles of wine. You bring the Tums.

IOU COUPONS for Mom

To:_____

From:_____

Date:_____

Reason:_____

Date Redeemed:_____

To:_____

From:_____

Date:_____

Reason:_____

Date Redeemed:_____

To:_____

From:_____

Date:_____

Reason:_____

Date Redeemed:_____

MOTHERHOOD MERIT BADGES

She gave birth to you. Give that woman a sticker, dammit!

Bless my buttons—you can mend!

You've been tested, and you pass.

That loan was a big deal (don't tell Dad).

Your cooking still rocks my world.

You make me want to phone more often!

You passed on some good stuff.

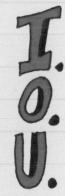

IOU COUPONS for Mom

I.O.U. →

HUNK MOVIE NIGHT

I've inherited so much from you, Mom: my mouth, my butt, my weird facial tic . . . but there's one thing that stands above 'em all. Yes, it's my unquenchable passion for hot famous dudes. From Cary Grant to Harrison Ford to Brad Pitt, you have some fine taste, woman, and I thank you for passing it on. So let's hit the multiplex and indulge that sweet tooth. Dad doesn't have to know.

LUNCH AT THE CUTE PLACE DAD WON'T SET FOOT IN

You: Oh my, look at that lovely restaurant.
Dad: If the guys saw me there they'd actually punch me in the face.
You: The flower arrangements are lovely.
Dad: There is a hoagie-meatball-BBQ-wings place right by our house.
You: Oh, look. They have low-calorie options.
Dad: The words "deep-fried" are no place on this menu.

OK, so I'll go with you to this joint, and Dad can get takeout.

A SHOPPING DAY

Listen up, Mom. You haven't aged a year. In old photos of you, I see your glowing smile, your bright eyes, and the exact same clothes from 1982. It might be time to leave the Polaroid-era memories in the album where they belong and get with the fabulous fashion of the now, for new pictures require some new attire. Let's hit the store and I'll snap some pics of you in the throes of a next-generation shopping frenzy, movie-montage style!

IOU COUPONS for Mom

To:_____

From: _____

Date: _____

Reason: _____

Date Redeemed:_____

To:_____

From: _____

Date: _____

Reason: _____

Date Redeemed:_____

To:_____

From: _____

Date: _____

Reason: _____

Date Redeemed:_____

LOST IN TRANSLATION— NO MORE!
A Size-conversion chart for Your Wallet

Hi, Mom,

AS YOU WELL KNOW, YOU DON'T NEED TO BE AN AMBASSADOR to get some clothes from out of the States. You don't even need to leave the comfort of your own mall! Foreign designs are all over the place—but like the menu at a sushi restaurant, I often have no idea what to order or how much I'm going to get. Here's a helpful little card to tell your fashion sushi from your fashion sashimi. Just find the clothing size you want to get, and locate the British or other European equivalent.

Your size _____ child, _____

U.S./EUROPEAN CLOTHING SIZE CONVERSION CHART

WOMEN'S DRESSES/SUITS

US	UK	European	US Letter
2	6	32	XS
4	8	34	S
6	10	36	S
8	12	38	M
10	14	40	M
12	16	42	L
14	18	44	L
16	20	46	XL
18	22	48	1X
20	24	50	2X

WOMEN'S SHOES

US	UK	European
5	2.5	35
5.5	3	35.5
6	3.5	36
6.5	4	37
7	4.5	37.5
7.5	5	38
8	5.5	38.5
8.5	6	39
9	6.5	40
9.5	7	41
10	7.5	42

FIVE REASONS WHY EUROPEAN CLOTHES ARE ALWAYS TOO SMALL

1. American designers add sizes to make up for the time difference.

2. Clothes put on bigger numbers to avoid getting kicked by Italy's giant angry boot.

3. It's a conspiracy to make Americans feel fat. Also, all of Europe is skinnier than you.

4. The clothes shrink in the salty Atlantic air in shipping. Not really.

5. Microscopic elves secretly shrink European clothes at night. Pests.

U.S./EUROPEAN CLOTHING SIZE CONVERSION CHART

MEN'S SUITS

US	UK	European
32	32	42
34	34	44
36	36	46
38	38	48
40	40	50
42	42	52
44	44	54
46	46	56
48	48	58

MEN'S DRESS SHIRTS

US	UK	European
14	14	36
14.5	14.5	37
15	15	38
15.5	15.5	39
16	16	41
16.5	16.5	42
17	17	43
17.5	17.5	44

MEN'S SHOES

US	UK	European
6	5.5	37.5
6.5	6	38
7	6.5	38.5
7.5	7	39
8	7.5	39.5
8.5	8	40
9	8.5	41
9.5	9	42
10	9.5	43
10.5	10	44
11	10.5	45
12	11.5	46

IOU COUPONS for Dad

I.O.U. — QUALITY TIME TOGETHER

Dad, I was listening to "Cats in the Cradle" yesterday (*whimper*), and it struck me that we haven't hung out in a while. Once upon a time, back in the days when I was a teenager brimming with evil, this was acceptable—desirable, even. Now it's just depressing (*sniffle*). So, let's have a drink and shoot the shit down at the pub. I'm sure we'll have a good time then, Dad. You know we'll have a good time then (*SOB!*).

I.O.U. — CAR WASH

Dad o'mine, there are three things you treasure more than your car: your marriage vows, your quarterback, and . . . nope, that's it. I mean, I'm sure you love me, but if you had to choose between your child and Ol' Honky . . . well, I'd go to the junkyard with my head held high.

In honor of that special father–vehicle relationship, please accept this humble car wash coupon. And may your car shine as brightly as the sun.

I.O.U. — YARD WORK

Father, Romans, countrymen, lend me your ears;
I come here to rake the lawn, not ignore it.
For the yard work that kids do lives after them:
The good is oft remembered by their parents.
So let it be with our green'ry. Noble Mom
Hath told me that it needs crazy tending, yo.
If it is so, I got it. No worries, Pop.
And happ'ly shalt you regard it, evermore.

IOU COUPONS for Dad

To:_____

From:_____

Date:_____

Reason:_____

Date Redeemed:_____

To:_____

From:_____

Date:_____

Reason:_____

Date Redeemed:_____

To:_____

From:_____

Date:_____

Reason:_____

Date Redeemed:_____

NEED SOME F.A.T. (FATHER ALONE TIME)?

Hey, Dad,

YOU CAN'T POSSIBLY remember the last time you didn't have somebody in your peripheral or all up in your face. It must feel like a reality show where everybody is constantly watching and you can't get your own moment off camera. Hang up this sign when you're fed up with the crew, and they'll go on a long, union-sanctioned smoke break.

Respectfully yours,

_____

DO NOT DISTURB

WHAT? WHAT IN GOD'S NAME ARE YOU DOING HERE? FOR THE LOVE OF PETE, I'M TRYING TO HAVE SOME FATHER ALONE TIME (FAT), AND I CAN'T HEAR MYSELF THINK WITH YOU PEOPLE BARGING IN ALL THE TIME. I'M A MAN, DAMMIT! A GROWN, INDEPENDENT, MANLY MAN, WHO OCCASIONALLY NEEDS <u>HIS OWN PERSONAL SPACE</u>. WHY, YOU ASK? DO I NEED A FRIGGING <u>REASON</u>?

(TURN OVER)

FINE. OK. IF YOU MUST KNOW, I'M:

____ WORKING! I DON'T COME TO
YOUR JOB AND BUG THE CRAP
OUT OF YOU, DO I?

____ WATCHING THE GAME, FER-
CHRISSAKES. AND SO HELP ME
GOD, IF YOU INTERRUPT ONE
MORE TIME, I'M GOING TO
SHOVE A HELMET UP YOUR
BUTT.

____ READING THE PAPER. DO YOU
HAVE ANY IDEA WHAT RUSSIA'S
UP TO LATELY? I DON'T
EITHER.

____ POOPING. WHAT? YOU ASKED.

____ STEWING IN MY OWN BITTER-
NESS. IT'S WARM AND COM-
FORTING, LIKE A BLANKET
MADE OF LOATHING.

____ OH, GOD. JUST LEAVE ME
ALONE, PLEASE. DO I REALLY
NEED AN EXPLANATION?

IOU COUPONS for Dad

SOME X-TRA READING MATERIAL

So . . . uh . . . . Dad . . . I guess we're both . . . uh . . . mature enough . . . to acknowledge that you . . . er . . . uh . . . um . . . have needs . . . Yeah . . . So, um . . . ee, I have this . . . stash, I guess . . . of Victoria's Secret catalogs . . . and, um . . . if you want 'em . . . . y'know, to order Mom a gift . . . or something . . . uh . . . they're all yours . . . OK? . . . . OK . . . I'm gonna go wash my brain now . . . and let's pretend we didn't have this conversation.

I.O.U.!

GARAGE/BASEMENT/ATTIC CLEAN-OUT

Once upon a time, in a fanciful suburban land, there was a glorious dad who was also a bit of a pack rat. Now, Dad's manifold piles were filled with wondrous, useful items, but they were getting out of hand. Fortunately, Dad had a most beloved child, who pledged to eliminate his vast accumulations of crap . . . er, treasures.

Then, everyone would live happily ever after.

I.O.U.

A WARDROBE UPDATE

Dad, it's time to face facts: Sweater vests, creased dungarees, and knee-high athletic socks do not a wardrobe make. That's not to say that Mom dresses you funny. It's just to say that your Cosby-inspired closet could use some updating. Whaddaya say to a relatively painless day of man-oriented shopping? I can't pay for it, but I can make it as tolerable as humanly possible. Because I love you, but I'd love you even more with a new shirt.

IOU COUPONS for Dad

To:_____

From:_____

Date:_____

Reason:_____

Date Redeemed:_____

To:_____

From:_____

Date:_____

Reason:_____

Date Redeemed:_____

To:_____

From:_____

Date:_____

Reason:_____

Date Redeemed:_____

DAD MERIT BADGES

Reward Dad for being a real trouper.

You didn't scare my date!

For keeping the road rage to a minimum.

You're a master of the grill!

Thanks for the loan!

I show off this DNA, it's so good.

We leave the lights on just to keep you busy.

IOU COUPONS for Grandparents

QUALITY TIME WITH YOUR GRANDCHILD

_____, you're my two favorite people in the whole world. (Don't tell Mom and Dad.) I love you so much, and this year, I want to spend as much quality time together as humanly possible. (Honestly, you'll be sick of me by the end of it.) So, you choose the day and time, and I'll bring the bingo and Lawrence Welk reruns. It'll be grand!

I.O.U.

YOUR LIFE STORY

There's nothing I love more than a long, involved story about the olden days. Because I admire how you walked uphill to school both ways during a tornado. And I love that your high school's single elective was Advanced Patriotism. And yes, it's HILARIOUS how your only toys were imagination and roadkill. Really, though, you need to write this stuff down. In fact, I volunteer to transcribe it for you! (It's what any patriot would do.)

TECHNICAL ASSISTANCE

I have sworn an oath to never reveal what you're about to hear. Kids today actually have a secret language. Cell phone, TV, computer, even coffeemaker and toaster instructions are written in code so those not in the know find them infinitely more complex than they need to be. It's all a conspiracy to get your money. Lucky you know an insider who will translate for free. Me!

IOU COUPONS for Grandparents

To:_____

From:_____

Date:_____

Reason:_____

Date Redeemed:_____

To:_____

From:_____

Date:_____

Reason:_____

Date Redeemed:_____

To:_____

From:_____

Date:_____

Reason:_____

Date Redeemed:_____

BIG DATE

"Why is a nice kid like you still single?"

"Darling, when are you going to get serious and get married?"

"You know, I'd like some great-grandchildren before the good Lord takes me."

OK, OK. I get the picture. And to get you off my case, JUST THIS ONCE you can set me up. I'll choose the day, the time, and the place, but you'll choose the actual date. If it works, I'll be forever grateful. But if it doesn't, we shall never speak of this again. Deal?

CHAUFFEUR FOR A DAY

"A badger ate my only pencil! Joke's on him, now he's got lead poisonin'!" That's what everybody in the old days talked like, right? "Everybody git on the wagon, 'cause we're off to town fer supplies!" You must have had to fight wild animals just to run the simplest of errands. Like, "We're outta beans and horseshoes, so git walkin'!" Let me treat you to a day of easy travelin'. I'll drive you anyplace you want, all day.

A DAY IN THE LIFE OF AN UNDERSTUDY ⇐

In the days of yore, grandchildren sat at their progenitors' knees, eager to soak up their valuable knowledge. Alas, those heady times are over, and now youths ignore their elders for the more immediate pleasures of vice and video games. I say, "No more!" Grandparent, I will learn your most treasured skill, whether it's pie baking, bridge playing, or speaking in the lilting tones of the old country. It will be bully!

IOU COUPONS for Grandparents

To:_____

From:_____

Date:_____

Reason:_____

Date Redeemed:_____

To:_____

From:_____

Date:_____

Reason:_____

Date Redeemed:_____

To:_____

From:_____

Date:_____

Reason:_____

Date Redeemed:_____

chapter 4

INSTANT GIFTS FOR COWORKERS

HOW TO KISS BUTT AND MANIPULATE PEOPLE

HERE'S A FUN THOUGHT: You probably spend less than two hours a week with your own mother, but forty-plus hours with coworkers. That means you know more than you cared to about Wendy's bunion, Jack's fourth midlife crisis, and Betty's failed affair with a puppeteer. Whether you like it or not, they know tons about you, too. Louise can name both your parents and eleven of your twelve first cousins. Bob knows you'd rather be touring with your folk band, Unicorn Barf. And thank god for Henry, who talked you out of marrying the heroin dealer. That would have sucked.

For better or worse, these folks are your office family. And every now and then, they could use a little pick-me-up. When Marie's reamed by the boss, use the Stapler Disguise Kit to transform her Swingline into a wild, paper-crunching crocodile. If Gordon the IT Guy teaches you PowerPoint, inflate his ego (even more) by dropping a Thank You coupon on his desk. And if Shelly gets fired? Well . . . there's actually not much you can do about that. But a Merit Badge might ease her crushing depression for a few seconds.

Of course, you can also give these gifts to coworkers who are genuine pals. Like a walking motivational poster, you'll remind them that the secret to SUCCESS is US.

SUCKING UP: A SUPPLY LIST

Remember how everyone felt when your grade-school teacher dimmed the lights and wheeled a TV and VCR into the classroom? Locating your coworkers' "break time" buttons will have the same glee-inspiring effect. You won't build a career solely as a pusher of caffeine, candy bars, and cigarettes, but it certainly won't hurt. Keep a suck-up supply list here.

COWORKER'S NAME	COFFEE (MILK? SUGAR?)	FAVORITE CANDY	FAVORITE SALTY SNACK	FAVORITE TV SHOW TO DISCUSS	FAVORITE PERSON TO BITCH ABOUT

IOU COUPONS for Coworkers

THANKS FOR YOUR HELP

Four hundred gallons of coffee. Four hundred thousand phone calls. Four million billion trillion copies. And still, you stuck it out. I've never met a person with as much resourcefulness, stamina, and ability to tolerate white-out fumes. For that, you have my admiration and respect, as well as my stapler. (Can I grab that back when you get a chance?) In your honor, happy hour drinks are on me.

CHEER UP

Aw, man. I know it sucks to be here right now. I know it's been rough going, and if you could choose any other job in the world at this very minute, Hardee's Toilet Scrubber would rank higher than this one. Cheer up, though, because it can only get better. The sun will rise. The flowers will grow. The client will choke on something. Don't forget: You're a fantastic worker, and if I could choose an Office Dream Team (and Shaq wasn't available) you'd be my starting center. In fact, let's get some lottery tickets so we'll remember how lucky we are to have you here.

GOSSIP QUEEN

In this dark, unending world of cubicle hell, you (and maybe the coffee machine) are my shining beacon of joy, hope, and limitless dirt. Like my own personal Off-US Weekly, I can always count on you for the lowdown about the boss's kids, the assistant's new boyfriend, and a certain coworker's "little problem" (*wink*). And for that, I salute you. Let's book a lunch meeting next week to go over the updates on your Who's-Sleeping-with-Who spreadsheet.

IOU COUPONS for Coworkers

To:_____

From:_____

Date:_____

Reason:_____

Date Redeemed:_____

To:_____

From:_____

Date:_____

Reason:_____

Date Redeemed:_____

To:_____

From:_____

Date:_____

Reason:_____

Date Redeemed:_____

TEH NOOB KEYBRD

These stickers can help a newbie find their way around their confusing keyboard. They're also good for dressing up a Mac keyboard (because Apple users love it when you mess with the look of their machines).

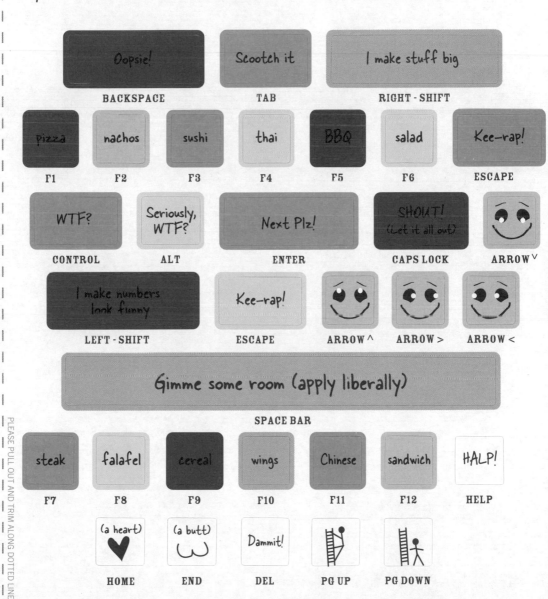

Oopsie!
BACKSPACE

Scootch it
TAB

I make stuff big
RIGHT - SHIFT

pizza
F1

nachos
F2

sushi
F3

thai
F4

BBQ
F5

salad
F6

Kee-rap!
ESCAPE

WTF?
CONTROL

Seriously, WTF?
ALT

Next Plz!
ENTER

SHOUT! (Let it all out)
CAPS LOCK

ARROW ˅

I make numbers look funny
LEFT - SHIFT

Kee-rap!
ESCAPE

ARROW ^

ARROW >

ARROW <

Gimme some room (apply liberally)
SPACE BAR

steak
F7

falafel
F8

cereal
F9

wings
F10

Chinese
F11

sandwich
F12

HALP!
HELP

(a heart) ♥
HOME

(a butt)
END

Dammit!
DEL

PG UP

PG DOWN

i.o.u.

THANKS FOR TIPPING ME OFF ON THAT FLASHY FEATURE IN EXCEL/POWERPOINT

I feel like I've been using a pencil to flip omelets over here. I can't count the days I've lost trying to fit an elephant into a wine bottle. I guess I don't need a car to squash a grape. Weird analogies aside: Thanks for the Excel/Word/Powerpoint/etc. tip! I owe you one.

THANKS FOR SAVING MY ASS

There was one seat left in the escape pod and you gave it to me. I was treading water in a poison jellyfish sea and you threw me a raft. The Lincoln Memorial was going to fall on me and you caught it and put it back after a good, honest spanking. Thanks for coming to my rescue in that meeting. I owe you big-time!

THANKS FOR HAVING MY BACK

When I was a kid two bullies squished an ice cream cone into my face and my friend Jenny just stared and did nothing. Since that day, I knew I needed tougher allies in the war on injustice. So, when you removed that proverbial Rocky Road from my visage and made me a proverbial sundae and let me eat it while you proverbially hogtied the proverbial bullies, I knew I'd found my for-reals teammate.

IOU COUPONS for Coworkers

To:_____

From:_____

Date:_____

Reason:_____

Date Redeemed:_____

To:_____

From:_____

Date:_____

Reason:_____

Date Redeemed:_____

To:_____

From:_____

Date:_____

Reason:_____

Date Redeemed:_____

WITNESS THE WILD SIDE OF A SWINGLINE

Transform everyday office supplies beyond recognition!

Is your colleague looking a little bored today? Here's a way to offer some diversion at the workplace: steal her stapler, staple remover, tape dispenser, and white-out bottle and use the stickers on the next two pages to transform these items into ferocious-yet-functional desk accessories.

TO CREATE THE STAPLEGATOR:

1. Stick the eyes right behind the rectangular "push pad" on top of the stapler. Follow the fold guides on the stickers and refer to the picture on this page to get the eyes to pop up, as intended.

2. Stick the gator tail on top of the stapler, behind the eyes.

3. Attach the nose to the front of the stapler and adhere the teeth to the silver sides of the staple trough.

4. Place two little feet on the front of the stapler base, and one foot on each side.

TO CREATE THE STAPLESTRICTOR:

1. Stick the eyes on the flared top of the staple remover, right above its fanged teeth (again, follow the fold guides and refer to the picture on previous page).

2. Adhere the snake tail to the top of the staple remover, behind the eyes.

TO CREATE THE HIPPO-TAPE-AMUS:

1. Adhere the eyes to the top of the tape dispenser, right behind the tape roll (follow the fold guides and the picture on previous page).

2. Stick the hippo's nose and teeth to the front of the dispenser, right below the metal serrated tape edge.

3. Attach the legs to each side of the dispenser.

TO CREATE THE CORRECTOR MONKEY:

1. This one is easy—simply adhere the monkey sticker to the front of a white-out bottle, with the cap positioned just above his head (like a hat).

NOTE: You'll also find captions for these creatures on the sticker sheets, which describe their natural behaviors in their desktop habitat.

STAPLER (AND STAPLE-REMOVER) DISGUISE KIT

Here we have a glimpse of the rare Staplegator, a vicious reptile native to the corporate jungle, known for organizing papers! And—oh my! Is that a Boa Staplestrictor? They abhor order and will stop at nothing to undo the hard work of the Staplegator. Let's watch as they meet on this remote desk.

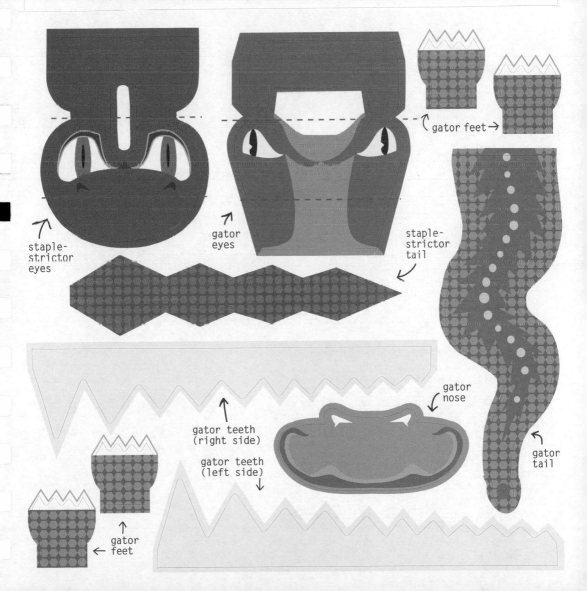

staple-strictor eyes

gator eyes

gator feet →

staple-strictor tail

gator nose

gator teeth (right side)

gator teeth (left side)

gator tail

← gator feet

TAPE DISPENSER (AND WHITE-OUT) DISGUISE KIT

We're truly lucky to find this Hippo—tape—amus away from its drawer habitat. Keep away from its toothy mouth or get taped up! Looks like a friend has arrived in a tree! The Corrector Monkey likes to fix mistakes, but don't sniff his bodily fluids. Toxic stuff! If we're fortunate, the two will put on a show right here.

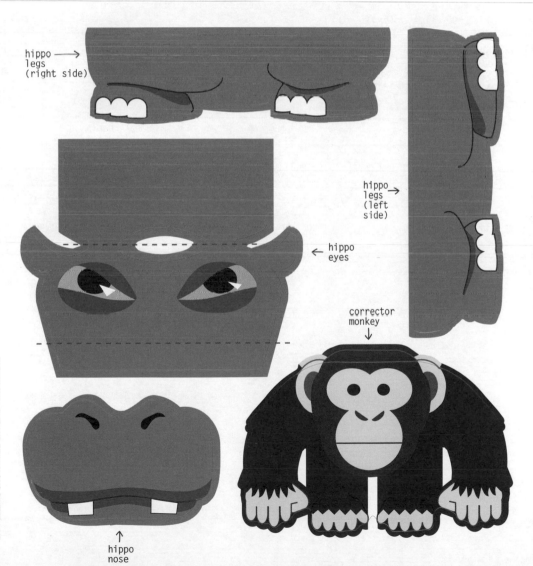

hippo legs (right side)

hippo legs (left side)

← hippo eyes

corrector monkey

hippo nose

IOU COUPONS for Coworkers

I.O.U. THANK YOU FOR YOUR GUIDANCE

If you look up "mentor" in the dictionary, it's located really close to "mental," which is what I would go without your guidance. It's crazy here, and I can't thank you enough. You're brilliant (like Einstein), patient (like Job), and sagacious (like Yoda), and I'm way lucky to have found such a stellar adviser.

I.O.U. THANKS FOR THE IDEA!

A haiku in appreciation of your awesome idea:

It made so much sense
I was totally like, DUH!
Now your name in lights

Thank you! I'll make sure everyone sings your praises, and may more poetry flow.

I.O.U. THANKS FOR THE IMPORTANT CONTACT

According to social theorist Malcolm Gladwell, there are people within certain cultures called "connectors." In a nutshell, these folks know fun people and connect them to others of interest. Recently, you did this for me, and HOLY GOD DID IT PAY OFF. George W. Bush didn't have this good of a connection to get into the White House. I'm in awe, and you now have permanent access to my Rolodex. Holla!

IOU COUPONS for Coworkers

To:_____

From:_____

Date:_____

Reason:_____

Date Redeemed:_____

To:_____

From:_____

Date:_____

Reason:_____

Date Redeemed:_____

To:_____

From:_____

Date:_____

Reason:_____

Date Redeemed:_____

COWORKER MERIT BADGES

Getting a sticker was a major incentive in kindergarten—
why should it be any different at work?

You collate like no one's business.

Thanks for keeping up the sweet supplies.

You rock that slideshow thingamajig.

You've got a formula for ass-kicking.

Thanks for fixing my paper jam.

Your magnetic field is deadly.

chapter 5

IOUs AND ACKNOWLEDGMENTS FOR ALL OCCASIONS
RANDOM PRESENTS FOR RANDOM PEOPLE

REMEMBER WHEN YOU GRADUATED FROM HIGH SCHOOL? And when you had your confirmation/bat mitzvah/quinceañera? And when you were born? Of course you do. And you probably remember all those awesome gifts you received as a result. Your family, your friends, and your dad's assistant spent a lot of time putting those presents together. They wanted you to be happy. And to get a raise from your dad. But mostly, it was the happy thing.

Now it's your turn. New generations of grubby cousins and dirt-poor college buds are taking monumental life steps, and it's your responsibility to support them as best you can. Fortunately, in the absence of money and actual thoughtful gifts, coupons will do quite nicely.

So, rip out some sentiments and start bestowing: Congratulate your best friend on his smokin' hot wife-to-be with the Engagement IOU. Use the Big Test certificate on your next-door neighbor when she finally passes the bar exam. Present your little brother with the New House coupon after he takes on his first mortgage, since there's nothing like telling a relative, "Hey, bro, I'll help you paint. Because your place looks like an Italian whorehouse right now."

Remember: They did it for you. Or they will in the future. And this way, you're guaranteeing those gifts are really good.

REUSE, RECYCLE, REGIFT

Regifting is certainly one way of handling an emergency situation, although it takes some degree of organization to pull off without committing the ultimate faux pas—presenting someone with a gift that they once gave to you. Don't rely on your memory alone. Log all regiftable items as you receive them, and keep tabs on your relocation program.

GIFT	GIVEN BY	REGIFT TO	DATE

IOUs AND ACKNOWLEDGMENTS
for all occasions

i.o.U. CONGRATULATIONS ON YOUR ENGAGEMENT

In human history, there's never been another engaged couple as perfect as you. Well, except Paul Newman and Joanne Woodward. But you guys come in a close, wonderful secon— Oh, wait: Mel Brooks and Anne Bancroft. Still, you're DEFINITELY the third–best couple on the face of . . . Ruby Dee and Ossie Davis. Forgot about them. Bogie and Bacall, too. Man, they're awesome. Anyway, congratulations on your . . . what was this about? I forget. But let's get drinks or something.

♥♥♥♥♥♥♥♥♥♥♥♥♥♥♥♥ ♥♥♥♥♥♥♥♥♥♥♥

CONGRATULATIONS ON YOUR FIRST ANNIVERSARY

I.o.U.
COUPLES WHO DIDN'T MAKE IT A YEAR: Helen Hunt and Hank Azaria (11 months), Jim Carrey and Lauren Holly (9 months), Carmen Electra and Dennis Rodman (5 months), Renée Zellweger and Kenny Chesney (4 months), Lisa Marie Presley and Nicholas Cage (3 months), Ernest Borgnine and Ethel Merman (32 days), Dennis Hopper and Michelle Philips (8 days). COUPLES WHO DID: You guys! YOUR PRESENT FROM ME: A romantic dinner for two at _____.

I.O.U.
FREE BABYSITTING
Oh my God. OH MY GOD. Are you . . . are you OK? Did you shower this week? You look like you haven't slept in three months. And on your face . . . is that vomit? I hope so, because the alternative is too awful to contemplate. I'll tell you what, New Mom. How about you take off for a few hours to rejoin the living, and I'll watch the baby. It's on me. Trust me, you need it. (P.S. Congratulations.)

IOUS AND ACKNOWLEDGMENTS
for all occasions

To:_____

From:_____

Date:_____

Reason:_____

Date Redeemed:_____

To:_____

From:_____

Date:_____

Reason:_____

Date Redeemed:_____

To:_____

From:_____

Date:_____

Reason:_____

Date Redeemed:_____

IOUs AND ACKNOWLEDGMENTS
for all occasions

CONGRATS ON YOUR NEW JOB!

Hear this, unemployed people: My favorite person is no longer among your ranks! That's right, you're trading unlimited freedom and The Price Is Right for deadlines, cubicles, and interminable meetings with HR! WOOOOO! On the bright side, you'll be bringing home an actual paycheck, and can finally visit a doctor to have that . . . thing . . . looked at. Plus, in honor of your accomplishment, let's have a power lunch. That's what people with jobs do, you know.

HOORAY, YOU'VE BEEN PROMOTED!

With great power comes great lunchability. Since you're all important and stuff now, tell your underlings that you're having a power lunch with some deep-pocketed

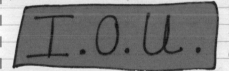

lobbyist, then get the hell out of there for some fun eats with me, my treat! Congratulations!

LET'S HEAR IT FOR RETIREMENT!

You've been digging and digging for oh-so-many years, and now your work is complete. Tell me, how bright is the light at the end of the tunnel? Can you describe it to me over a game? Poker, chess, hearts, board games, Mega-WWII-War-Strategy 3.1—name your favorite and I'll pretend to lose, anytime you like. (Except weekdays—since some of us still have jobs!)

IOUs AND ACKNOWLEDGMENTS

for all occasions

To:_____

From: _____

Date: _____

Reason: _____

Date Redeemed:_____

To:_____

From: _____

Date: _____

Reason: _____

Date Redeemed:_____

To:_____

From: _____

Date: _____

Reason: _____

Date Redeemed:_____

THANKS FOR LENDING ME YOUR HOME

Hi! I was staying here at your lovely place while you were away. Yes, I was naked the whole time. The big couch is cozy, softer on the left cushion than the right. The hot tub's been warmed up, so to speak. I wouldn't recommend lying naked and wet on the kitchen floor, though. Talk about chilly! Don't worry about your windows; they all open wide, you can see the neighbors, and rain comes right in when they're open. So they work! Your digs are great, and I'm happy to house-sit anytime!

CONGRATS TO A HIGH SCHOOL GRADUATE

Graduating means you can pilot a sailboat, right? Oh. Maybe it was heart surgery. You're a heart surgeon. No? Bagpiper? Lion tamer? Garbage taste-tester? Triathlete? Insect photographer? Eighties-television critic? Used-wrapping-paper salesman? Tackle-box designer? Polka-band roadie? Eh, whatever you are, let's go see a movie. My treat.

CONGRATULATIONS ON EARNING YOUR GRADUATE DEGREE

Did you know that 97 percent of Americans with postgraduate degrees become billionaires? Also, studies show they're constantly surrounded by supermodels, and all but a few survive to the age of 120. What's more, Girl Scout cookies often magically appear at their doors, along with king-size glasses of chocolate milk.

OK . . . these are a tad fabricated, but here's what's real: I'm getting that diploma framed for you. Trust me, the supermodels will love it.

I. O. U.

IOUs AND ACKNOWLEDGMENTS
for all occasions

To:_____

From: _____

Date: _____

Reason: _____

Date Redeemed:_____

To:_____

From: _____

Date: _____

Reason: _____

Date Redeemed:_____

To:_____

From: _____

Date: _____

Reason: _____

Date Redeemed:_____

CONGRATS ON YOUR NEW HOME  i.o.u.

It's a big day, my friend. You're leaving the land of the apartment dweller and moving into your own home. Beware, though: With great closet space comes great responsibility. Walls will need painting, faucet valves will need tightening, and the neighbor's kid will need $20 to mow your lawn ($30 if he's entrepreneurial). To get you started, I'm happy to pitch in. You name it: painting, packing, whatever. I'll be there, and I might even bring beer.

IN HONOR OF YOUR  COLLEGE GRADUATION

What the hell? You weren't supposed to graduate! Do you know how many bets I've lost with this one? I had you dropping out the second year. And THEN, you graduated in less than seven years, which throws my side bet out. I thought the odds were stacked in my favor, and wholly against yours. Sigh. Is this an OK time to borrow some money? Aren't recent college grads stocked with cash? Let me take you out to dinner and we can talk about it.

I.O.U. CONGRATS—YOU PASSED THE BIG TEST!!

The late nights . . . the piles of notes . . . the last-minute study sessions, when you feverishly crammed your sleep-deprived cranium with fact after semiuseless fact . . . they finally paid off. You passed. And you didn't even need to hire that kid to take the test for you. (Um . . . you didn't hire her, right?) Anyway, way to go! I'm proud to know such a humongous geek. To celebrate, let's get coffee. At a bookstore, of course. I want you to feel at home.

IOUS AND ACKNOWLEDGMENTS
for all occasions

To:_____

From:_____

Date:_____

Reason:_____

Date Redeemed:_____

To:_____

From:_____

Date:_____

Reason:_____

Date Redeemed:_____

To:_____

From:_____

Date:_____

Reason:_____

Date Redeemed:_____

chapter 6

HANDY-DANDY GIFT CARD HOLDERS
SPECIFIC SENTIMENTS FOR UNSPECIFIC PRESENTS

WHAT'S A MAN WITHOUT A WELL-TRIMMED BEARD? Or a woman without fabulously dangly earrings? Or a baby without a bear hat? What's a fine dinner without a sprig of parsley topping it off? Or a Lexus without a sparkly purple bow? Or a stripper without rainbow-hued glitter shoes?

What's a gift card without something to dress it up a little?

Oh, you might think gift cards are cute already, with their gleaming plastic lacquer and pleasingly rounded edges. Some even have gorgeous modern fonts and professionally centered text. Still, they're nothing—NOTHING, DO YOU HEAR ME?—without fancy punch-out holders festooned with appropriate sentiments.

Why? Well, you can't POSSIBLY give a Coffee card without expressing yourself about espresso. You can't dole out Food Court cards without waxing poetic about waxy potatoes, either. And of course, there'll be no Sporting Goods cards without dedications that are both sporting and good. (We don't know what that means either. Just go with it.)

Sure, the gift cards themselves are thoughtful. But going that extra mile—with nonspecific text written by people you've never met—will show you really care.

Happy giving!

INSTRUCTIONS

How to Use These Gift Card Enclosures

1.

Procure a gift card directly from a retailer or select one from a rack of gift cards at your favorite convenience chain store (Rite Aid, Walgreens, CVS).

2.

Discard the ugly generic packaging (if any) that comes with the gift card.

3.

Punch out the gift card holder that best suits the sentiment and purpose behind your gift.

4.

Slide the corners of the gift card into the slits in the holder, fold it along the score lines, and seal it with a sticker (included at the very back of this book).

Oh! Hey! You know what you'd look really, really good in? Clothes. No, seriously. I mean it. Shirts could totally be your thing. They'd complement your torso well, I think. And pants? Pants would make your legs look so, so . . . leglike. And let's not even start in with socks. I can't imagine anyone pulling them off as well as you. Especially paired with shoes. Seriously. In fact, in honor of your big day, I'd like to buy you a shirt or some socks or something. Seriously, it'll be awesome.

IN OTHER WORDS, I HAND-PICKED THIS GIFT CARD FOR YOU BECAUSE:

_____

_____

_____

_____

_____

_____

_____

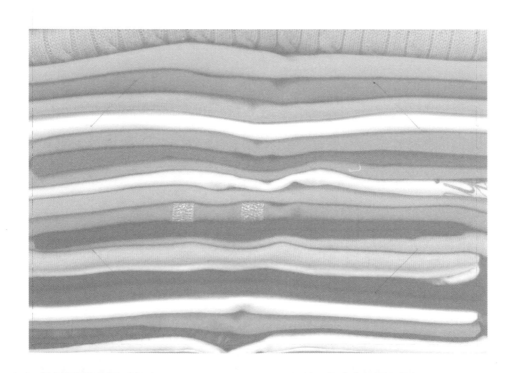

Yo, with all your gear, you must be making something radical in your living room. Methinks with just a little more power, your monstrosity will live! More little lights! More dials! More buttons! A winky little LCD here and something that ejects there! Less wires (yeah right)! It's alive! Use this gift card to make your technopower wet dreams come true, but keep it clean and benevolent to mankind.

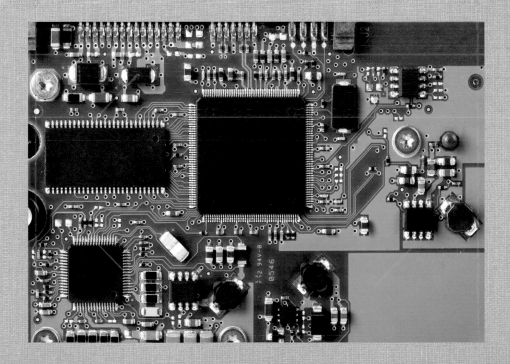

IN OTHER WORDS, I HAND-PICKED THIS GIFT CARD FOR YOU BECAUSE:

_____

_____

_____

_____

_____

_____

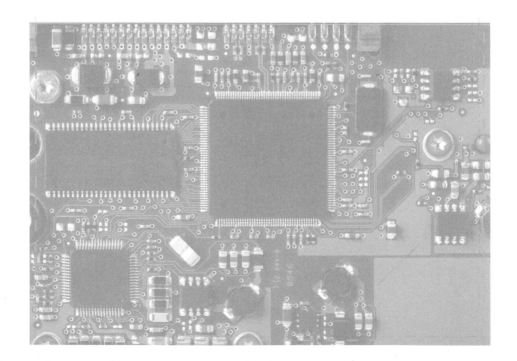

Show me those jazz hands! NOT JAZZY ENOUGH! I want to see some pizzazz, some panache, some pampering! Your fingers could use an upgrade, and I want to be blown away. Go get yourself a nice touchup at the salon, and come back to me with your best routine. Cover 'em up with unicorns, NASCAR, glittered glitter, a dragon hologram, a portrait of Obama, whatever you think it'll take to set my senses sizzling!

IN OTHER WORDS, I HAND-PICKED THIS GIFT CARD FOR YOU BECAUSE:

_____

_____

_____

_____

_____

_____

_____

I have a friend who goes to the cute holiday vendor tents downtown and steals ideas. She sees something cool, figures out how it's made, then goes home and makes it herself. But to get to that point in her craftiness, she needs stuff. A lab, gear, Elmer's glue, safety scissors, googly eyes, pipe cleaners, and uhhh . . . that's all stuff that crafters use, right? Or am I thinking of second grade? Anyhow, go make!

IN OTHER WORDS, I HAND-PICKED THIS GIFT CARD FOR YOU BECAUSE:

_____

_____

_____

_____

_____

_____

A great, great man once said: "Reading is totally awesome, so you should do it a lot with a lot of books and sometimes magazines, but mostly books because that's where all the literature is. And if you can get books with big print and pictures, even better, because then you can read more books a lot faster and people will think you're really smart and stuff. Has anyone seen my keys?" Truer words hath never been spoken, so please accept this gift card from me for a bookstore. That guy would have wanted you to have one.

IN OTHER WORDS, I HAND-PICKED THIS GIFT CARD FOR YOU BECAUSE:

_____

_____

_____

_____

_____

_____

Call me crazy, but I'm pretty sure if we secretly replaced your blood with Folgers Crystals, you wouldn't notice. Hell, you might have even done it already. In honor of your extreme, perpetual caffeine jones, I present you with this gift card, which will keep you in warm joe for . . . well, at least the rest of the day. It's redeemable at any location, but . . . uh . . . you probably have to peel yourself off the ceiling first.

IN OTHER WORDS, I HAND-PICKED THIS GIFT CARD FOR YOU BECAUSE:

_____

_____

_____

_____

_____

_____

_____

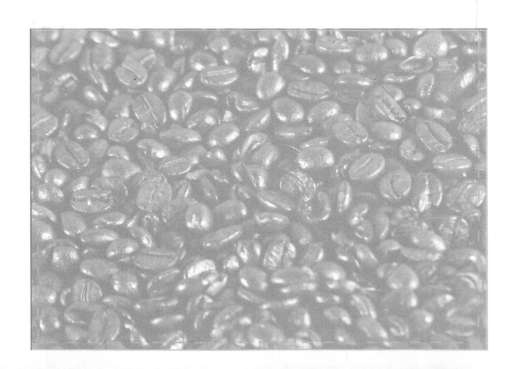

You know what they say: There's nothing like a huge supply of hardcore, totally illegal narcotics. And with this drugstore gift card, you can purchase as many as you like. Because that's what they sell at drugstores, right? Mom was all like, "Uh, hon, I don't think you can get those kind of drugs at a drugstore. I'm fairly sure it's a place for toothpaste and tampons and such." But I'm all like, "Nuh-unh! I know what a drugstore is!" So here you go! Go to the drugstore! And don't forget to share when you're done.

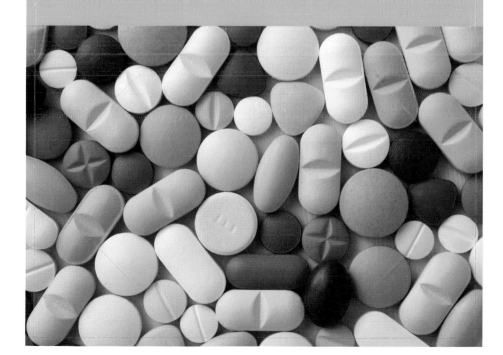

IN OTHER WORDS, I HAND-PICKED THIS GIFT CARD FOR YOU BECAUSE:

_____

_____

_____

_____

_____

_____

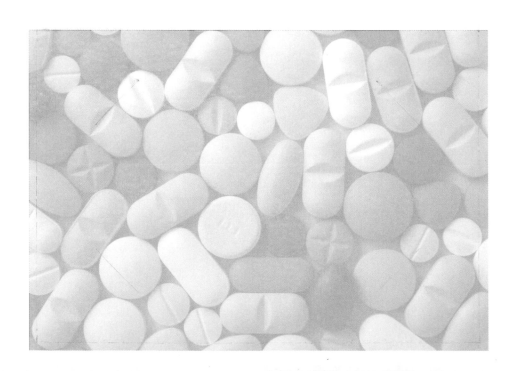

Millions of shoppers agree: The whole reason for hitting the mall isn't perusing Pacific Sunwear, Chess King, or four different kinds of Gaps. It's the food. Places like Cinnabon, Jamba Juice, Applebee's, and Wok & Roll fuel the American retail experience, allowing us to both maintain our momentum and shut the kids up for a few minutes. Supporting these fine eateries is our imperative as hungry citizens. So go forth and slurp, my friend. Orange Julius and Uncle Sam will thank you for it.

IN OTHER WORDS, I HAND-PICKED THIS GIFT CARD FOR YOU BECAUSE:

_____

_____

_____

_____

_____

_____

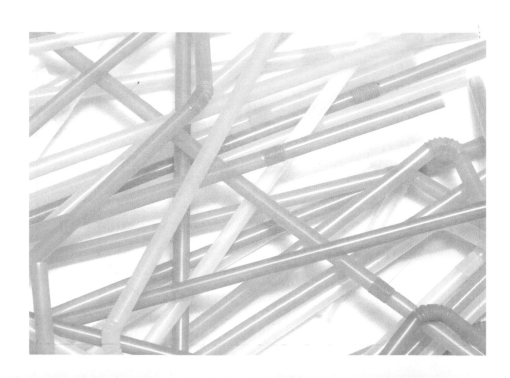

I love when a gift is REALLY specific. So here it is, the most specific gift in the world. I knew exactly what you would want. It wasn't easy! I went through your mail, called your friends, tracked your Web browser history, got your credit report, took a trip to Hong Kong, and bugged the lamp next to your bed. Here it is! The one gift that perfectly hits the mark, completely tailored to your preference. You're welcome. I can call off the private detectives now. (Well, at least you can pick out whatever you REALLY want.)

IN OTHER WORDS, I HAND-PICKED THIS GIFT CARD FOR YOU
BECAUSE:

_____

_____

_____

_____

_____

_____

_____

I love when a gift is REALLY specific. So here it is, the most specific gift in the world. I knew exactly what you would want. It wasn't easy! I went through your mail, called your friends, tracked your Web browser history, got your credit report, took a trip to Hong Kong, and bugged the lamp next to your bed. Here it is! The one gift that perfectly hits the mark, completely tailored to your preference. You're welcome. I can call off the private detectives now. (Well, at least you can pick out whatever you REALLY want.)

IN OTHER WORDS, I HAND-PICKED THIS GIFT CARD FOR YOU BECAUSE:

_____

_____

_____

_____

_____

_____

_____

STICKER SEALS FOR GIFT CARD ENCLOSURES

To: _____

From: _____

To: _____

From: _____

To: _____

From: _____

To: _____

From: _____

To: _____

From: _____

To: _____

From: _____

STICKER SEALS FOR GIFT CARD ENCLOSURES

To: _____

From: _____

To: _____

From: _____

To: _____

From: _____

To: _____

From: _____

To: _____

From: _____

To: _____

From: _____